NOTES ON SILENCE:

a songwriter's
musical guide
for the Trump era.

for all students and fans
of music,

regardless of: gender identity, race, class, sexual orientation, color, military status, sex, religion, creed, national origin, ancestry, age, veteran status, disabilities, or genetic information.

Preface to the Contents.

I

TACET

II

TACET

III

TACET

~John Cage, 4'33"

CONTENTS.

Author's Preface.

It's Time to Zero The Board.

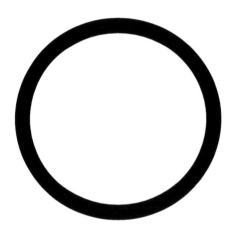

Chapters Within.

PART ONE:

SCALING THE MOUNTAIN

CHAPTER ONE.

An Intro to Nothingness.

The Blank Canvas Is the Air.

Each something starts from nothing.
This book could have been nothing.

On a musical staff, there is more blank page
than notes and rests.

BLANK-

NESS

A Note is a Something.

Two somethings make a duality.
Three somethings a triality.
Four, a quadrality. etc. ad infinitum.

But for the student of music,
we start with nothing first.

The blankness.

Empty mind.   Empty ears.

On the relationship between nothing and something.

The nothingness supports the somethingness.

A note appears on a blank page.

While we can have nothingness without somethingness, we can't have its reverse: somethingness without nothingness.

Even if all the notes stopped, we wouldn't have total nothingness.

(but we can get close...)

A poem.

Here is water. There is land.

N   O   W

do   you   understand?

CHAPTER TWO.

The Substance of Nothing.

A Thought Experiment.

Can you listen to nothing?

Try to listen right now.

What do you hear?

...Can you describe the sound
without using nouns?

In an An-echoic Chamber.

In a room treated to have no sound,
you will still hear at least two sounds.

1. The sound of your nervous system.

2. The sound of your own bloodstream.

Nothing, meet music.

Nothing is an abstraction of the mind.

We can conceptualize it,

but can't

experience it

in sound.

Even so,

it's a very important word

in the study of music.

Should I play a note?

Deciding to play a note is a big deal.
It's putting something into the nothing.

You should decide to play a note
only
if you believe in it.

Reasons why
I might play this note.

i.   I find this sound to be interesting on its own. It's morphology, or physics, peaks my interest.

ii.   When I listen to you play your note, I like how this sound combines with yours. Heard together, it makes a new, bigger, exciting note.

iii.   In the context of this song, and the images and feelings it gives me, this sound adds to the communication of the meaning of the piece.

iv.   In the context of this series of songs we are performing tonight, this sound is evocative, emotionally powerful, and expressive.

v.   In the language of our band, this sound
     helps us continue to reinvent ourselves,
     by challenging what we think is beautiful.

CHAPTER THREE.

On Hearing Nothingness Everywhere.

When musicians stop playing.

All notes and noises are somethings.

When musicians stop playing,
those sounds can be heard.

To those ambient sounds of the environment,
intentional,
or non-intentional,

we

are

listening.

When musicians stop playing,
is the sound still beautiful?

CHAPTER FOUR.

On Listening with Others.

At the limits of hearing.

What is audible to us is limited by our hearing range.

When we reach that limit,
though we may no longer be able to hear the sound,

others may still be able to hear it.

Likewise,
sounds that are within our spectrum,

others may not be able to hear.

Nothingness is relative.

Play with time.

All sounds have a length. When it appears, it is said to attack.

That peak is its birth.

When it disappears, it is said to decay.

That is its death.

A sound can decay (or attack) either slowly or quickly.

Can you make a sound that attacks quickly and decays slowly?

Now can you make its opposite: a sound that attacks slowly and decays quickly?

How long did the sound last?

Musicians have fun playing with time.

Transitions between songs.

What is contained by music?

When a piece ends,

there is time

before

the next piece

begins.

That time between   pieces
is also part of what we call
music.

Repetition.

No sound ever repeats itself exactly.

No moment is ever exactly the same.

The sonic environment is unpredictable.

What will emerge after the next silence?

Musicians
use form

to play
with this
idea.

No sound ever repeats itself exactly.
No moment is ever exactly the same.

Cosmos.

Dear Creator,

When I make a sound,
do I create
a new planet
somewhere in the galaxy?

Let me know soon.

Love,

Jeff

CHAPTER FIVE.

Open Ears and A Wide Open Mind.

Living music.

Movement and interaction between musician and audience through sound can bring about transformation. The direct and intense communication cuts through our humdrum everyday experience to profoundly affect us.

Have you ever been to a show where you felt that your mind and spirit had experienced an abrupt and discrete leaping from one plane of thought to another? Where suddenly you felt you could understand the words transcendence, catharsis, metamorphosis, transmutation, deliverance, emancipation, birth and death, maturation, and mind expansion? Where paradigms shifted, portals opened, and the line between tragedy and comedy blurred? Where you experienced sensory overload and the music seemed to enter at every pore of your body, and all at once?

I experienced that while watching Leonard Cohen play.

Warming up checklist.

- o Sightlines.
- o Stage exits.
- o Temperature of instrument. (it needs to warm up, too)
- o Last row in the audience.

Pre-show tuning.

Pre-show,

tune your instrument,

tune yourself,

and tune the room.

Where is the center?

Walking onto the stage.

All sounds are holy.
The stage is our holy ground.

Every sound we hear,
made or not made by someone on this stage,
is equally important.

The incidental quiet sounds become part of
the music.
The shuffling of the crowd. The cough. The
smoke machine.

All singing and humming along.

The center becomes everywhere.

Empty the mind.

The process of unlearning.

Forget theory of.
Forget tradition of.
Forget technique of.
Forget history of.

music.

The Possibilities of Sound.

o Location within a stereophonic sound field.
   Phantom Image.

o Length. Duration.

o Attack and Decay.

o Rhythm. Articulation.

o Morphology. Texture. Timbre.

o Tone Colors.

o Resonance.

o Effects and Parameters.

o Overtone Structure.

o Building, setting up, the circuit.

o Intensity.

o Relative Volume. Dynamics.

o Amplitude (average and peak).

o Reflections.

o Frequency.

- Melody. Harmony.
- Routing.
- Signal Flow.
- Scenes. Change over time.
- Ideas. Interpretations.
- Phrasing. Form.
- Emotions.

How hot or cold is it
right   now?

CHAPTER SIX.

Jikan.

Change, the only constant.

As in life, so in music.

No difference.

Dedication.

This book is

dedicated

to the memory

of

Leonard Cohen.

Jikan.

These are *Killingry.*

You are what you have.

Don't you want this?

Isn't this who you wish you were?

underSTAND THE DIFFERENCE

PART TWO:

REACHING THE PEAK

CHAPTER SEVEN.

Return to the Blank Canvas.

TACET

PART THREE:

DESCENT FROM THE MOUNTAIN

CHAPTER EIGHT.

Get Out of Its Way.

low stage.

Audience and performer are the same.

All part of the same wave.

No definite centers.

masking.

Sounds may mask one another
when one sound
is layered
upon another sound.

Consider getting out of its way.

six rapid questions.

I

If you adjusted immediately, would you
still call it an error?

II

Why

   do

      you

         think

            it's not beautiful?

III

Communicate the text,

and the subtext

might come out.

IV

Have you considered the noise floor?

V

Is there a melody?

VI

*How can one something
be more important
than another something?*

CHAPTER NINE.

Negative Space / Positive Void.

Expansion Beyond Music.

dynamic systems.

Each something is something in motion,
from a transmitter to a receiver.
For example, music moves at 1100 ft/sec, the
velocity of sound in air.
It moves faster or slower depending on the the
temperature and humidity, and the type of
medium its passing through.

A musician plays a note.

The string vibrates,
and the charged air is sent hurling towards the
audience.

Their ears receive the sound;
their brains interpret the sound into feelings.

a dynamic system in action.

natural dynamic systems:
the air we breathe.

The flow of oxygen and carbon dioxide
between plants and animals illustrates the same
kind of dynamic system as in music.

The oxygen animals depend on is released into
the air by plants as a byproduct of their
photosynthesis.
Likewise, the carbon dioxide plants depend on
is a byproduct of animal's respiration.

Both plants and animals are transmitters and
receivers.

We co-evolved.

Clean air is a relationship, a connection,
a dynamic system of interaction and exchange
between plants and animals.

flow within the system.

The mountains formed through tectonic and
volcanic forces.
The inner core of the Earth is solid. Mostly
nickel.
The resonance frequency of Earth is 7.83 Hz.

At the end is the beginning.

Everything set into motion is still in motion.

Try to be still.

equilibrium reached.

We are all transmitters and we are all receivers.

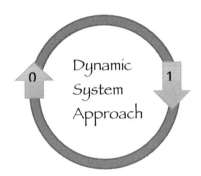

0 Dynamic System Approach 1

these get routed, all the time,
all around Earth.

Water.

Air.

From place to place.

Knowledge.

Music.

Weather.

2   8

Electricity.

(the exchange)

Light.

Information.

Money.

Soldiers.

Love.

Lava.

CHAPTER TEN.

Shared Air:
Music and Politics.

What contains music?

Music is part of cultural production, or Livingry.

Livingry, as opposed to Killingry, focuses on seeking humanizing laws, or, laws that recognize the dynamic systems of Earth, the equality of all its sentient life forms, and their basic rights to to live peacefully and musically together.

Livingry	Killingry
Environmentalism	Nuclear war
Peaceful Resolution of Conflict	Fossil Fuel
Public Health and Safety	Global Arms Trade
Poetry, Ethics	Corporate Media
Local Music Scene	Fascist Government
Meditation, Integrity	Disaster Capitalism
Mindfulness	Slave Labor
Friendship	Sex Trade
Electricity	Addictions to: pills, caffeine, sex, alcohol, gambling, guns
Free Press	Unregulated Financial Sector
Elected Officials	Global Free Markets
Independent Court	Biased Courts
Democracy	Conflicts of Interest
Diplomacy	Irresponsible Behavior
Love, Community	Revolving Door
Humanism	
and more…	

LIFE

IS

SO

MUCH

BIGGER

THAN

YOU

THINK

No Jews

No Blacks

No Gays

Allowed

another example of Killingry.

CHAPTER ELEVEN.

Keep The Whole in Your Head At All Times.

From Nothing to Something, and Back Again.

get in the zone.

When you're in it,

You play everything perfectly.

Not just tone elements,
But all elements together.

Perfect prayer.

All elements of grace

accessible

and within reach.

easy.

Making Music

Is

Like Setting CLOCKS

On   On   On
   and   and
and
   Off   Off
       Off

.

create the flow.

Setup the atmosphere where creativity can thrive.

The piece that took fifty years to perform just ended.

a note can be any sound,
with any length.

Delivered with,
Originality.
Attitude.
Conviction.

be an advocate for living music.

a passion for listening.

French	entendre
Spanish	oír
Italian	udire
Portuguese	ouvir
Rumanian	asculta
German	hören
Dutch	horen
Swedish	höra
Danish	høre
Norwegian	høre
Polish	słyszeć
Czech	slyšeti
Serbo-Croat	čuti
Hungarian	hall
Finnish	kuulla
Turkish	duymak
Indonesian	dengar
Tagalog	marinig
Russian	slishat
Greek	akou'o
Arabic	yasmaa
Hebrew	schamah
Yiddish	heren
Japanese	kiku
Swahili	sikia

cultivate an open, beginner's
mind.

a tonal experiment.

What happens
when I
Hit something really hard?

and then

What happens

when I

Hit the same thing

now

really

soft?

CHAPTER TWELVE.

The way is still open.

the way is open.

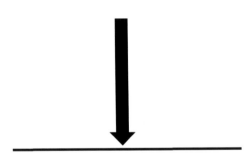

The next moment is never scripted.

And there is always more to learn.

to-do list.

- Give gifts.
- Visit the children's hospital.
- Smile.
- Visit the elder home.
- Make music.
- Call your parents.
- Read.
- Cook for others.
- Sweep the house.
- Pet the dog.
- Pet the plant.
- Listen right now.
- Meditate.

CHAPTER THIRTEEN.

Techniques for developing the musical touch.
Putting something into nothing.

finding the touch.

The musician's touch is

first and foremost --

a touch of the mind.

sensitive, gentle, caring,

giving, empathic, and kind.

If you can feel it in your heart,

that's more than half the battle.

a poem.

a musician's touch

Is like smoke.

taking on all shapes and forms.

rising and disappearing. It

dissipates   into   nothingness.

Or,
like tumbling
under water,
wrestling with the current.

Or,
like the wings of a bird
O u t s t r e c h e d.

developing the touch.

In our first lesson,

We will pet a dog.

Then later,

We will pet a plant.

Further advanced studies will have us

Sit in silence.

And finally,

We will sit in silence,
while we imagine

petting a dog and a plant.

gravity.

Though the hands are our furthest extremity,
it is with the wrist, shoulder, and back
that we find the gravity in the touch.

Body light and nimble, like mind.

If it must become louder,
Shift more of your weight into the note.

a poem.

To be like the sky.

Wide open to receive all possibilities.

Or like the sand.
Both ancient and just being born.

Blue scatterings of sunlit atmosphere.

Unbiased by high-net-worth individuals.

Created by the trillions of inhalations and exhalations

of the millions of species of plants and animals

Occupying Earth,

Through eons. eons. eons. eons. eons…

breathing.

In – take from the plants.
Out – give back to the plants.

Mindful that my breathing has a tempo,

Aware that my heartbeat syncopates my breathing.

In – deeply, 3 counts, 1 , 2 , 3.

Out – slowly, 3 counts 1 , 2 , 3.

Find your breath, and the touch
will find itself in nutrient rich soil
to grow.

let it go.

The book is almost done.

Let it go.

Make music today.
Listen to the world.

The Unstruck Sound has Unlimited Tone.
~ no instrument needed~

Just a big heart.

You have all the answers,

and all the questions you need.

THE END.

also by this author:

The Music of Living. ruminations on
the meaning of life, astronomy,
evolution, and music.

When Money Grows on Trees. a
fable for young and old.

16274426R00102

Printed in Poland
by Amazon Fulfillment
Poland Sp. z o.o., Wrocław